invisible me

a poetic journey to loving myself

DONESSA ARAPI

The Invisible Me by Donessa Arapi
Copyright © 2019 All rights reserved.

No portion of this book may be reproduced, stored in a retrieval system, or transmitted in any form or by any means, except for brief quotations in printed reviews, without prior permission of author.

Book Creation & Design
DHBonner Virtual Solutions, LLC
www.dhbonner.net

Tender Flower Press
ISBN: 978-1-7340329-0-1

Printed in the United States of America

This book is **dedicated** to Me...

For the **courage** to **write**
from the depths of my **soul**

Contents

Letter to My Younger Self 6
Fading 7

BROKEN

Why do I always have to be the ugly one? 10
Generational curse 12
Writing 13
Help! 14
Oops 16
Cry Baby 18
I can't do this 20
Body Image 22
Happy 23
People don't want to hear 26
Self-Hatred 27
Shattered Pieces 28
Sex Slave 30

BREAKTHROUGH

Conversations with a therapist	36
Fat Girl	37
An Aged Woman	38
My Joy	40
Blinded by Me	42
Who Am I	46
Breathe	47
Days	48
I Am…	51
Inner Peace in Me	52
Inner Peace in You	53
Flower	54
Future	56
Accept Me For Who I Am	57
Angels	58

Letter to My Younger Self

Dear Donessa,

    I love you. I know you feel alone and scared. Don't, be afraid. You will be fine. You are safe. (tearing) God has a purpose for your life. You are not invisible. What you are unable to see? God sees. So, come out into the light. People may laugh, but so what? They judge you, but so what? I know no one seems to understand you. I know it seems like they just bark at you. Yes, you are different and that's ok. (tears) Its not a bad thing. You are special! Not weird, God made you to be different because He has a plan for you. Stop hiding. Come let me hold you close, and you will be safe.

    The child in Donessa is crying. Donessa, the adult is also crying. I see you sit by the window with so much on your mind. Let it go. Be free, you don't have to be sad. Lay your head on me. I will help you find your way. You will be fine.
    I kissed the younger me.

    Maybe that's why I hold children so close, so they can feel safe too.

Fading

No more will you see
Me
Hide behind the great oak tree

Fearing to be what God birth in me

Deeper in the woods I would run
Beneath the twigs and leaves the Son would come
Giving me life to breath and believe

That I am free to see what's inside me

I will show my face and replace
The frown that drown my beauty and grace

No more will I be
The invisible me

Giving Thanks

Thank You, Lord
for allowing me to enjoy the simple things in life.
Blue skies
Ocean too
Warm gentle breeze
Green trees
Sun rays
Hope for everyday

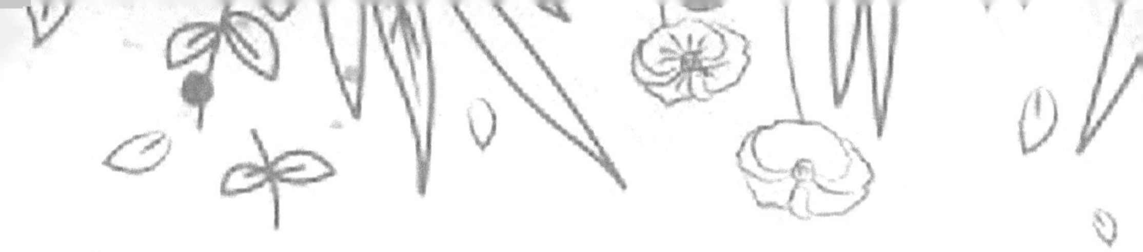

broken

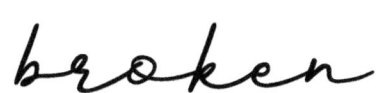

"My worth is more than I think."

—RFA

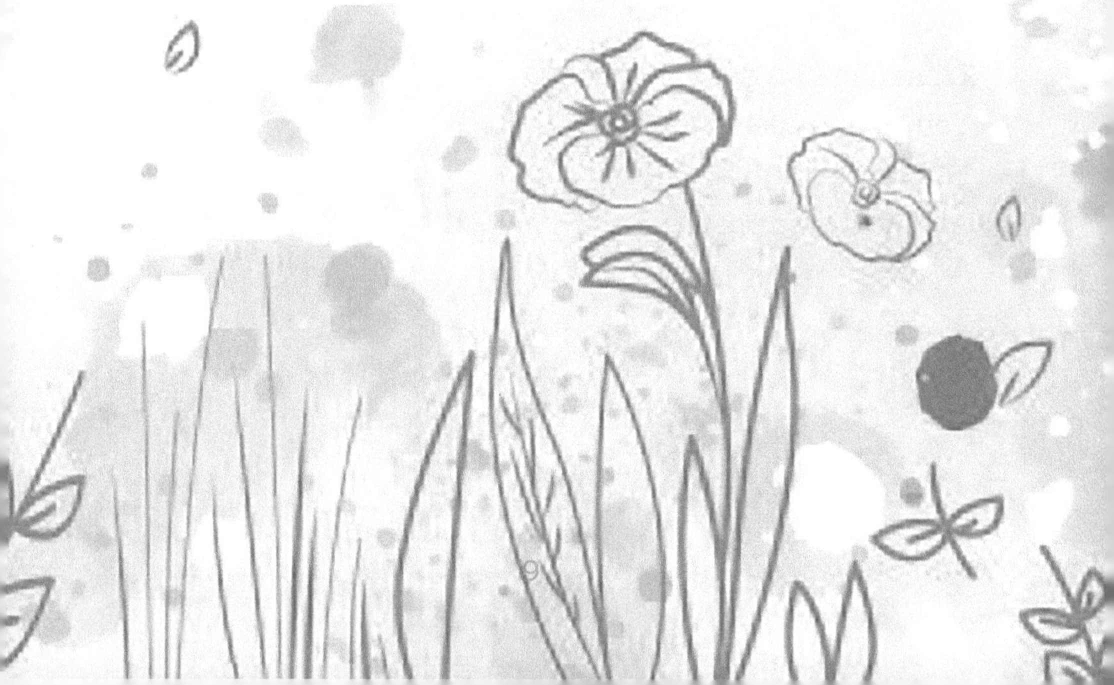

Why do I always have to be the ugly one?

Picked over. Looked over. Passed over never once looking into my eyes
Getting the leftovers
I'm not the prize
After they can't have who they wanted
They look my way for a little taste of my sweet tea
But you would never officially choose me
Because you feel there's sweeter than me, smoother than me, more desirable than me

Oh yeah, I hear people say, "Girl, you shouldn't think like that."
You are beautiful in your own

What the hell does that mean?
You have a nice smile
You are friendly
And, oh so supportive

As they look me up and down trying to discover where my worth lies
Sometimes, if they really know me, I'll get a "you're so creative."

Will somebody tell me, "why do I have to be the ugly one?"

Chump change
Second best
Servant
Discount shelf
Wall flower
Only when needed
This is the life of the Ugly One

Generational curse

When master comes, covers your face and does his busy
Leaving a mess upon your chest
Feeling like a slave even in these days
Jumped upon
Dumped on
Dumped in
Used and abused
Now, they've emptied their boat
Stroked your throat
Choking on their creamy float
They rest
While you suppress the feeling of emptiness

Writing

I wished paper aligned the inner walls of my head. Every thought would splatter and be captured.
I lay down and new thoughts emerge. I feel the stroke of my pen. Yet, my laziness wins.
Time moves fast. Death is approaching. I die every day I don't create.
My drive is low. My purpose is stagnated.

Will I become a part of the riches place on earth?
Where is that, you ask?
According to Miles Munroe it is
"The cemetery"

Will my gifts go unseen?
Will my words mean anything to anyone?
Will these papers be trashed once my body is burned to ash?

Let the smoke fill the air that it may carry my words everywhere.

Help!

This is a familiar feeling. I've lost direction. A vicious cycle of too many thoughts and a lack of motivation. I keep looking for someone to fish me out of this murky pond. Its filled with self-pity, tears and defeat. If not blocked, it will be joined with a lack of self-worth.

God's image
Jesus' life
Yet, I'm still not free.
My walls are decorated with affirmations.
Seeking the positive side of me

Yet, I'm still not free.
The destruction lives within me.
It wants to hang me from its tree.
Free falling
Free falling
Falling
Free

For as long as I can remember, I've felt invisible.
Never understanding that I wasn't
Nor was I born to be
invisible.

Tell the story:

When I was younger, I was scared beyond scared.
If that makes any sense?
In school, I would literally try to hide behind the child
who sat in front me. I didn't want the teacher to call
upon me to any answer questions.
I believed that I wasn't noticeable.
This feeling I've carried throughout my life.

Oops

Another one
Will I ever win this battle that is within me
Putting a stop to every move I make
Relationships bloom
Like cut flowers in a vase, they die
Raking away every start I try

I should come with a label
Warning:

Run as fast as you can
Before my energy destroys
No man can withstand
The fight of my pain
Just sorrow and rain
Nothing to gain

Silly guy
Could not see
Just happy to be
Feeling
Chillin
Dealing with me
Flirting you see

He wants us to be
We shall see
My heart fluttered
Mind went straight to the gutter
We played with each other
Building heat
My sweet
His meat
Our treat

Until the ugly showed itself
Lurking
Always ready
To throw rocks in my head
Confusing and reclaiming
My invisibility

I've taken the loss
Of many loves
And future tossed
Low self-esteem blinded my charm and gleam

I want to be free
Here's the door
You may not have my life anymore

Cry Baby

Why do you cry over people and their temporary existence in your life?

They were never yours.

The things that are

Do they not deserve your tears, heartache and suffering?

You give place to the emptiness, but no value to what is right before you.

Why must your tears be used to wash the pain that are oceans away?

When they should be used in the rivers that are here today.

True feelings are to be hidden.

No.
I believe expression is vital to one's
breakthroughs and healings.
Set the captives free

Unapologetically Me

I can't do this

Don't waste time knocking on my door
What do you see
Why call me

My demons won't die
They stay and walk by my side
Forcing me to cry

Leave
There's nothing to see here
I'm old
The best part of me used to be
Destruction laid it's claim bonding me to never be unchained

I did my best
Trying to impress
The youth of you

To finesse your caress
Oh, yes
I was passing the test
Braless
Laced
Moaning in the right places
No shame

Just fun and games
Seducing you to me

Sexy to my eyes
Miles I would fly
In search of happiness to be free... me to you

Body Image

My body is not beautiful
Stop with the lies
Stop trying to convince me to convince yourself to make me believe
All you want is to be pleased
And squeeze between my knees

Lanes and lanes of varicose veins
Driving me insane
They have overtaken my legs
Leaving me only with pegs

What geometric shape has my body to take
Circle, oval, triangle
Am I a fruit
Pear, apple or plum

Seeking to identify me

With eyes like a panda black you see
Hands like a map charting past journeys
Hair departed with the winds of time
Arms dangling from carrying life's heavy loads

Please do not try to convince me

Happy

Happy
Not
I've tried
I've lied
I've smiled in faces while my insides searched for far-away places

Helpful
Oh, so very careful to make sure others are loved and cared for
Wanting to feel it for myself

A caretaker
That's me giving a boost, a cheer, a listening ear
I'm just here
Yes, I know the Lord—don't get me wrong
He is the only one that keeps me strong
drugs
alcohol
food
porn

I'm a phony portraying
HAPPY

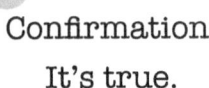

Confirmation:
It's true.

The mind is very powerful. What you believe, you believe.

Here's the story
I had eaten healthier and exercised for three weeks. Though, weight loss was not very visible. I could see and feel the inches that had melted away. My belly deflated, clothes complimented my body and sexy was knocking on my door.
A night out on the town drew me to further conclude that I was on my way down the weight chart. I felt good therefore; I looked good and established that I was attractive.

Let's take it a step further.
A pursuer of my flesh was given the rare opportunity to see my curviness in its entirety. I challenged myself to myself. My flaws and doubts could not hold me. Fighting through fear to find my freedom nothing nor anyone could contain me. I convinced myself. I was desirable and sexy in this ever-desperate journey for self-love.

Yet.
My pursuer, asked about my friends. I questioned his interest and was told "it was for informational reasons." He reassured me; it didn't mean a thing. Huh, then why know?

I questioned. His statement, "one is attractive. The other looks younger than you."

The wind escaped from my body.
I attempted to slap down my insecurities.
Throw them out the window of my mind.
But his words were planted like seeds and had taken root in my worth.
It seems there's always room in my core to store the ugly gloom.

Crash
And just like that
Weeks spent building and convincing me to love me
Wiped out with one blow.
How could that be
Was my mind misleading me

Powerful and brilliant
The mind
What controls the mind

Choice

People don't want to hear

Sometimes I want to die
I can't even cry
I pray and ask God why
I know it's by my own that I feel this way
It's hard to carry the load
The burden
Trying to discover, rediscover and activate
Is there freedom from being in the flesh
Are the burdens lighter after death
Count your blessings, "they say"
And I do
However, right now I am blue
The load I carry feels like a ton or two

By the way, how are you?

Self-hatred

It's not because of the color of my skin
I love that I am brown
It's not my hair
I love my curly kinky wild hair

It's my suit in which I live
My shame
No game
The original design I cannot decline

    Plump apple
   Large droopy thighs
    Black eyes
     Big top
    Little bottom
   Breast laid to rest

Granted I did a lot of damage to my myself
Filled it with unhealthy junk that can kill
It's not easy skin to live in

     Belly top
     Belly flop
     Belly drop

I've tried to hide
Even cried
My vessel of empty pride

Shattered Pieces

Today, I learned just how broken I am. It hurts to feel this way at the age of 53 about something that happened when I was 18. Who knew the long-term effect that it would carry throughout my adult life? Affecting every part of my being and the decisions I would make.
The mental, emotional and social aspect changed me forever. It was so crippling that I would never see myself as whole.
Not to mention, what I've done daily because of it. The self-inflicted pain and torture, shattered esteem and ego, dreadful tears of feeling unloved. Unable to distinguish the difference between love and lust in relationships.

How do I recover from this? Where do I find the strength to dig deep into my soul and find healing? I've searched before, but to no prevail. Surely, one day I will have peace within my spirit. No longer do I asked, why did this happen to me? I now need to find the pieces that were taken and replace them with self-love and healing.

No one can help me rebuild this structure, but God. Lord, help me not to be broken. Help me as I'm drowning in my despair of shame and ugliness. Help me to feel not as a failure, but a woman of strength and beauty. I can't seem to find the person you've created the jewel within.

Help me to shine and not be afraid of the person I am. To stop hiding behind emptiness and invisible screens. Help me to find my worth and value. Help me to stop putting myself up for sale for the bare minimum. Help me to stop fighting and the killing of Donessa.

Who you've called from the heavens above? Most of all help me to overcome this before I leave this earth. So that I may live as you have called me to live.

For once I want to believe that I am the prize and others are blessed to be a part of my life. Dry the rivers that flow down my face as I question my existence.

I want to live.

Sex Slave

I do for you what you ask of me
I want to please you
For I am not new and far older than you
Something attracted you to me
What could that be
Now you are asking me
Not to be
Me

Who do you want me to be
Your freaky sex slave
An image of your fantasy

So, you can have your way with me

"The problem is people are being hated when they are real and are being loved when they are fake."
—*Bob Marley*

Baby I love you

I love you the way you are

So you say

My vision of me

Fat
Curvy
Ordinary
Curly hair
Gap tooth
Sexy full lips
Dreamy eyes

Your vision of me

Fat
Curvy
Sexy
Exotic
Red lipstick
Straight hair

In this world, there are many issues that an individual will encounter in their lifetime. We are often chained by restricting factors.

"For I know the plans I have for you," declares the Lord, "plans to prosper you and not to harm you, plans to give you hope and a future."

-Jeremiah 29:11 NIV

A hard-protective shell
Carried well
Head to toe
Catching every blow
Delicate insides struggling to survive
Keeping all things alive
Building the pride
Not believing the lie
That I was told

Judgment is harsh

breakthrough

"Even through my broken, I have breakthrough."
—Bridgett C Farris

Conversation with a Therapist

"When did you first feel that you were invisible," asked the therapist?
The woman looked off into the distance. "I can't recall." Her eyes gazed through the window as if the answer would soon pass by. The therapist then asked, "do you feel that people can see you?"

"Of course," replied the woman! "This therapist must think I'm crazy,"
thought the woman.

"I know people can see me, but I can't see myself."

> "I knew you before I formed you in your mother's womb. Before you were born I set you apart and appointed you as my prophet to the nations."
>
> -Jeremiah 1:5 NLT

Fat Girl

Fat Girl, you are all that
When I look at you
OOOO WEEE
Sexy powerful and free
No wonder the haters hate
They can't take the radiance you make
Every time
Mouthwatering, Voluptuous
Pride in every step of your stride

Fat Girl
Fabulous Woman
Phenomenal Woman
Woman of essence
Thank you for being you
Thank you for allowing me to see
That I can be me
Intelligent Beauty

A natural cutie

An Aged Woman

I am old
I've told you
You must understand
As you journey across my bodily land
Your hands
Will cover grounds that are no longer sleek or meek
They will not glide across a terrain that is smooth or firm
They will; however, touch life's experiences
You will be exposed to the trials, struggles and strengths that have shape
My soul
You will understand the rhythm of my curvy domain

          Every roll
          Bump and
          Creek will tell a story

It will share how imperfection is made perfect in one's travels
You will come to know unconditional love and compassion in its purest form
You will partake of the girl I once was and the woman that I've become

        My innocence will touch you
        My experience will thrill you
        My wisdom will intrigue you

So, when you encounter an aged woman
Remember, you are among greatness
And when you love me
You love the world

My Joy

I've looked to many for pleasure
I've sown into endless relationships
The love
passion
support
wisdom
hope
humor
my Body
Only to receive the smallest effort returned
All empty vessels of what used to be

So, I sit here with no one to love but Me
And for the first time
This feels right

No one can fill this space
No one belongs in this place
No one can love me like Me

It was here all along
Covered by the hurt and pain, disappointment, abuse and negativity
My sweet beautiful smile
Cheerful and radiant
My full luscious body

Warm and inviting
My love powerful and unique

It's always been Me
I could not see
The core of my joy was living inside
Ready to do its work
Overtaking all aspects
Shining brightly
To love all that makes me

My Joy

Blinded by Me

I could not see
What you wanted from me
Genuine
Pure
Were your ways
But for days I insisted that you proclaim your hearts intent

Though, I was not content with your words
Because in me there was no peace
Seeking only me and my pleasure you would convey

But
I would make you pay for the way I had grown to hate me each day
It drove you away
My words of dismay for my body
Stripped away the light you once seen

I could not see
Until you set me free
All you wanted from me

Was me

"You were born an original.
Don't die a copy."
—John Mason

Why do I sit here pretending I am a writer?
I'm not pretending.
I am a writer.
In fact, I am an author.

I write about my

Feelings

Thoughts

Love

Pain

Beauty

Desires

Experiences

Truths

Visions

and anything else that comes through my door

Who Am I

I am life
Life is not me
I was born to be free
Yet society captured me

Dictating false beliefs
Of who I should be
Nearly killing all that the Creator made in me

You see
I am the trees strong and sturdy
I am the wind that carries the seed of love and possibilities
I am the ocean wide and endless
I am the whisper quiet and gentle
I am the rain that cleanse the pain
I am the storm powerful and loud
I am the skylight limitless and bright
I am the birds free soaring high above what is below me
I am the music full of emotions touching the hearts of others
I am nature a beautiful creation authentic one of a kind body soul and mind
I am words
I am beautiful

I am beautiful words

Breathe

Sometimes I forget to breathe

Not my normal breaths which God breathes for me

But deep breaths

The kind that pushes the junk inside of me... out

Holding me

Biting me

Scolding me

Filling my head with clouds

Strangling me with smoke

Trying to prevent me from ... being ...Me

Time to let it go

My trash can is full

There is no more room

So

Breathe

Breathe

Breathe

Days

Some days I
    Walk with confidence
    Some days I fall into disparity
Some days I
    Am radiant
    Some days I am dim
Some days I
    Am strong
    Some days I'm fragile
Some days I
    Am voluptuous
    Some days I am fat
Some days I feel sexy
        Sexiness
        Dripping sex
        Everywhere I go
Some days I am dry

Some days I
> Am words
> Some days I am silence

Some days I
> Am electrifying
> Some days I'm numb

Some days I
> Am love
> Some days I am anger

Some days I
> Am a fighter
> Some days I've been beaten

No matter the day
No matter which way
I am always Donessa

Fighting to find inner peace
That I may finally accept and love me

I Am...

I am older and younger at the exact same time.
I am happy being the vibrant sexual me.

I am a progressing work of art in God's hands.

I have a way with words like butterflies in an open field.
I spread my wings and fly.

Inner Peace in Me

I connect to the beauty of my natural environment

Like a tree strengthen by the wind
So am I
Grounded and rooted covering others
In all kinds of weather, I stand the test of time
Though, I may lose a few leaves here and there
And my branches may fall to the ground
I never stop growing and showing how profound I am
My trunk is thick with years of experience
They are shapely with curves from having to bend
I have bumps and scratches where people have climbed me
Dents and broken bark where I've carried others
And though, beautiful trees surround thee
There is not one like me

For I am wonderfully and fearfully made.

Inner Peace in You

Inner peace cannot be identified just by looking at someone
It may not be found in their eyes or heard in their words
Nor in their beliefs and interpretation of life

Inner peace cannot be given to you by someone's touch or actions
Stop looking to others for your core power

Inner peace is the breath you breathe
The oxygen that cleanse your soul as it enters your body
Release the negative
Inhale positive vibes
Search for the beauty that dances inside
Welcome the mellow aura of your quiet spirit
Let it arise

Inner peace is loving the you that is you
Without judgement or condemnation
Fear or bondage

Inner peace must be discovered, uncovered and birthed

Flower

I

am a beautiful flower
Planted by the Hand of the Creator
Watched over by the Holy Spirit
Watered by the blood
Nurtured by the Son

Wide open fields
Lavender appeals
Storms that would kill
Soil dry
Raindrops from the sky
I will not die

Future

Wherever I go
This I know
I will grow

Accept Me For Who I Am

I have
The power to brighten your day
The gift of hugs
The passion of love
The strength of steel
The heart to feel
The heartiness of laughter
The rage to fight
The mind to understand
The vision to create

And a beautiful spirit to behold

Angels

My angels up above
Filled with life and love
Forever watching me
Always protecting... you see
Where would I be
Without the light you give to me

I miss you so much
Daddy, Momma, Dinea, Darius,
Grandma and Granddaddy
I hear your cheers
You move through me

Just like yesterday
I see the replay
The laugh, laughter, laughing
Nothing can stop the love in my heart

When you left
A part of me did too
But the memory of each of you
Makes me brand new

The end is never the end
It's only the beginning
For something new

www.ingramcontent.com/pod-product-compliance
Lightning Source LLC
Chambersburg PA
CBHW060343080526
44584CB00013B/900